Solidarity.

Written and illustrated by
CHANEEN SALIEE

Copyright © 2020 Chaneen Salako

All rights reserved.

ISBN: 9798630878922

Dedication

To the women who raised me.
To the women who uplift me.
To the little women who made me a mother.

CONTENTS

Acknowledgements

The women mentioned in the poems at the end of this book have inspired me in profound ways, and many of them, I have never even met. I felt a pull, something inside of me wanted to acknowledge them in a permanent way because they have impacted my life monumentally, simply by being themselves: Maria Betsworth, Mimi Ikonn, Africa Daley-Clarke, Sunshine Abou Bakar, Candice Brathwaite, Lillian Jamfar, are some among many reasons why this book is in your hands. May it do for you, what they have done for me.

My Mother, who has always supported me and on one night in particular saved my life, is a woman to be reckoned with. She has been through life, really been through it but she always pulls through with sheer love, for us, her children, and for everyone.

My Nany, whatever she says I believe. Since she believes I can do anything, I can – do anything. Thank you, Nany for always believing in me.

Jasmine and Ocean my daughters who are making me cry as I write this. They make my heart swell and explode with joy. Thank you for making me slow down and experience peace while propelling me into my power. I love you.

I love you all.

INTRODUCTION

I've written Solidarity for women to know that they are not alone in the emotions and experiences they face after becoming a mother. The book is sectioned into four collections; Fluctuations, Perspectives, Gratitude and Solidarity. Each section will move you through the book as if on a journey and open up a conversation around some of the more taboo topics that we rarely discuss as a society.

Feel free to share individual poems with loved ones if you need to open up about how you feel but you're not sure how.

I hope that the vivid descriptions in these pages will help mothers, mothers-to-be and loved ones to understand that these feelings, as difficult as they may be, are normal and common and they do not last forever. Whether you read through this book chronologically or you dip in and out occasionally, I hope that you find solace in Solidarity.

I wrote most of these poems during times of intense emotion and at the time I never intended to share them with the world, but here we are. As I have begun sharing, I've learned and I believe that many of you will resonate with the emotions present in this book and I hope it will help you to work through and enjoy your journey.

Fluctuations

Fluctuations is the section of the book that deals with the more harrowing, numbing and difficult emotions that a mother may experience.

I've depicted such raw emotion in these pages so you know you're not alone if you experience similar feelings. They're also here to inform those who've been fortunate enough to avoid such emotions – to show them that these feelings are reality for some of the women and people in their lives.

I've tackled these difficult emotions at the book's beginning so as to pave the way to the light. Many women experience these emotional difficulties in early motherhood, amidst ever-shifting hormones and super-dependent babies. But it does get better.

As you work your way through this book, trust that you'll find your way to the light.

You've Come So Very Far

You see that smile upon your face
Sometimes it will grow
And other times
That smile will fade
When you're feeling low.

You'll feel euphoric
Watching your babe
And then emotionally numb
You'll question how you got to this place,
But the answers, they may not come.

So you'll hide away
Because 'life's a disgrace
You're the only one.'

This is not true,
I'm telling you,
I've been right where you are,
Take time today, to remind yourself,
You've come so very far.

Postpartum Pardon

You'll cry a lot
You'll keep it a secret
Until another mother
Shows the deepest,
Darkest,
Places within her mind
And you'll try to detach,
You'll try to be kind.

 "Extreme thoughts,
They say
It's commonplace"

But never
Ever
Will you feel like you can say
What your extreme thoughts are
Just in case
'They' come and snatch your babe away.
No.
No.
Let those thoughts go.

That smile upon your face will grow
And other women will comment on your glow
And a surge of hormones will course through
your body and your bones
And you will know
Because the change in your emotions,
And your thoughts, in your soul
Will be dire, dramatic,
Beyond problematic

That smile upon your face will grow
And then with the smallest woe, it'll go
And the way you see the world will change
From those first moments with baby
When you're all ecstatic
To this moment right here
That feels traumatic
Because you dropped your biscuit in your tea
And you can't see
How life can ever be
Okay again
And it doesn't make sense
Because you didn't really want the biscuit
Or the tea
And you're crying and weeping on your knees

When all you really want to do is sleep
But you're all alone
And baby won't …
He or she won't go to sleep
He won't properly feed
And you think back to when you agreed
To do this 50/50
You think back to before you conceived
But you're on your own
Again.

That smile upon your face will grow
And it'll go
And at times you may need to borrow
The smile on the face of others
To fuel your own
But that smile, that smile upon your face
Will show up again and again

And your babe will know
You love them.

4 am

Sleepless nights and sleepless days,
We had another 4am start today.

Throughout the night,
It's like a game
We play;

One will wake up
And one will go down

And on we continue,
Round and round.

Our time will come, though
Where we'll sleep right through

But until then here's a reminder for you:

If you can't get to sleep
For one reason or another,

Take a moment to rest
And recoup
Away from your role

 As 'mother'.

Anxiety

I'm trying to catch my breath
But there is no time
And there is no space
Simultaneously
There is so much time
And there is so much space
That it hurts my heart and makes it ache
Because I can't understand
How once again
I am in this place.

I cannot breathe, so my heart pumps harder
More beating.
More movement.
More life.
And the faster it goes
Or
Maybe it doesn't,
I think to myself,
But it just feels that way
Because in this moment,
 I am not well.
"This is not normal,

Something's not right"
The depths of me shout out
In the midst of this plight.
This is not normal,
My hands,
They shake.
Something's not right,
I'm not okay.
Breathe, they said.
So I try to breathe.
Leave, I say.
But I am not free.

I cannot go,
There are two baby girls,
They need their mummy
Because there is no one else.

Snap out of it.
It's the fight or flight.
There's something on your mind that's making
you fright.
But you're okay, girl!
 Yes, you are.
Take to your feet and sway side to side.

Yes, you'll ignore the baby as she cries,

But *you* need to be okay before you wipe her eyes.

Breathe in and pull out your phone,

Open up your notes,

Write a poem.

It's your way to find peace again

Then you can carry on, and only then.

I take a moment for me

And

I'm grounded again.

I am okay.

Close Call

I'm not sure I'll be able to sleep tonight
The incident of today
It'll haunt my dreams tonight
So instead I'll stay awake
Because I am terrified
To once again
Feel the heartbeat
 Of the stranger that held me tight
To once again
 See the sea of faces that held you,
And your sister
As I cried
I'm terrified
To hear the screech of the tires
As I saved your life.

Yeah, I probably won't sleep tonight
But that's okay,
 Because I'll hold you tight
And I'll feel your heartbeats
And see your faces
And we'll be alright
We are the lucky ones   29719

Silent Nightmare

It's in the silence of the night
That I feel like I'm done.
The feeds are endless,
Each minute lasts so long,
They turn into hours
And
Within seconds
I've gone,
From feelings of awe
To feeling so raw,
Like feeding is a chore
That I cannot do
 Anymore.

It's in the silence of the night,
I'll be feeding forever.
When will this end?
Never. Never!
The rest of my life
Revolves around this moment
I'll be feeding till I die,
I send myself a condolence,

In the silence of the night

There is no one here
It's just me,
All alone
With my worries and my fears

There is no one here
To tell me otherwise.
To tell me not to worry
To tell me to rationalise.

There is no one here
To explain what I know
To help me to see
How quickly they grow
And even sooner than that
How fast each moment goes.

It is in the silence of the night
That I am already done,
The feed is over,
It didn't take that long,
And once again
I've already gone
From feeling so raw
To feelings of awe,
As my baby begins to softly snore
And I scold myself for not enjoying this more.

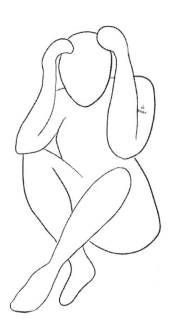

Justly Tired

It only feels this way because I am justly tired.
I remind myself that if I look at the clock
I'll realise I've only been feeding for 10 minutes.
To say that I don't need a clairvoyant to know
that this feed will be over within the hour.
So instead I say, "It's not the baby's fault. Don't
take it out on her." Then I say, "for God's sake!
It's 4am it's been an hour and you still haven't
finished. You still haven't burped. But it's not
your fault." And upon unlocking my phone with
my face I click through to Instagram because
Facebook is boring and YouTube is too noisy. I'll
just take my mind off this shit and see what's out
there in the world. And then I think, for f***s
sake, what am I doing? I'm only waking myself
up more. But if I wake up more, then I can bear
with this, but if I stay tired I can fall asleep soon.
Soon? Why do I put that pressure on us, on this
moment? If she stays awake forever I'll be okay
with that, I'll be calm because that the only way
to get through these forever moments.

I have this conversation in my head for a while. And then she burps and then she falls asleep and then I call myself silly for making this experience a shitty one when I should know better by now. I could just look at her, smile and appreciate that she's healthy.

I lay little baby down in her Moses basket to sleep. I lie down, I turn over and I begin to sleep. And it feels good and I feel blessed, lucky, happy, excited even. And I'm drifting off, like Iggle Piggle in that boat. Then I hear, like a shrilling siren in a Catholic Church during silent prayers, "Mama!" and I know what sort of day will lie ahead of me. I only have 2 hours left to sleep before it's light outside, but now baby girl is awake and is ready to battle.
The spiraling inside my head will continue and this time, I will not make it.

TV Parenting

I tried today
I really tried
But in the end
I cried
I cried

You came to find me
And I couldn't see
Your face
Through the tears
Which frightened me
And filled you with fear

So you cried today
We really cried
I bit my lip
A compromise

I turned to you
I dried your eyes
I'd pause the tears
Again I'd try
To love you hard

And soothe that fear
And grin at you,
From tear to tear

From ear to ear,
I mean
Ear to ear

See look at me
I cannot be
...
I cannot even speak

I can barely see
I just need time
Time to breathe
"I'm sorry baby
Go watch TV"

I Can't

I can't keep this up
And I can't ask for help
And if they can't really tell
Then maybe this hell
Isn't that bad!

I Cried Last Night

I cried last year, because of pregnancy.

I smiled last year, because I heard baby's
heartbeat.

I cried last month because she wouldn't eat.

I smiled last month because I got time to breathe.

I cried last week because she's getting teeth.

I smiled last week because I drank hot tea.

I cried last night because I don't feel free.

I smiled last night because she cuddled me.

Tired As Fuck

I'm up
I'm up
I'm up once again
Tired As Fuck
And in need of a friend

I'm up
I'm up
I never did sleep
It's taking its toll
It's the fifth time this week

I'm up
I'm up
And baby's half way to ten
I feel so alone
When will this end?

I'm up
I'm up
It's my first night
Yeah I'm a bit tired
But I'm feeling so bright

I'm up
I'm up
But just for tonight
Hubby's turn tomorrow
But I'm dreading the light

I'm up
I'm up
You can talk to me
I'm online right now
And I'm starting to freak
I can't really tell
If baby can breathe

But I need a friend
I'm in need.

When She Cried

And she cried

And I told myself she'd stop soon

And she cried

And cried

And I said,

This is not what I'd usually do,

Let you cry so much,

And she cried

But they say to ignore it

And it started out fake,

The cries weren't real

But somewhere along the way

She changed it,

She cried

The tears, they became real

She cried and cried

And I thought that if I give in now

She'd have won

So she cried

My way, responding to this was driving me insane,

So she cried

I tried,

I tried to be gentle and attentive always

But now

She cried

So I'm trying a different approach

But she cried and cried and cried

And I couldn't hear my thoughts

As she cried

I felt sick to my stomach

Wishing it didn't have to be this way

And she cried and cried

And I visualised

The beach

I visualised her not crying

And it didn't work

Because she was crying

She cried

A shrilling cry

And then before I knew it

I cried

Covers pulled up over my head,

Ignoring her fake cries

And now here I was

Silent tears streaming down my face

She cried and cried and cried so much

She just wouldn't stop crying

Sense of Security

It was on a rare occasion where I was relaxed, asleep even, when she came Storm Trooping in. But I did not hear her. She clambered upon the bed beside me, and then I did hear her and feel her all at the same time. She tore the covers away and plunged her fist into my dreams and removed me. My first thought was, is this real?

I was still asleep when the crying began, it was like a shrilling siren on a silent night, a night where you felt at your safest, wrapped up warm and in love, and then out of nowhere, this siren comes along, cold as ice, sharp like a knife, it tears through you, through your covers, through your illusion of safety, through your skin and right through to your nerves.

My nervous system was alight with fire. No, not fire, that sounds too romantic. It was alight with acid, biting through me, destroying any sense of security I ever had. Any sense of security I ever will have.

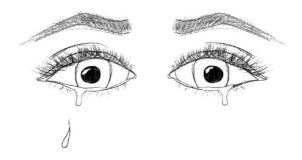

Perspectives

In *Perspectives* I take social norms, expectations and patriarchal ideas and smash them with beauty.

Perspectives features poems and prose that highlights the truth behind all the fear, hatred and disappointment we feel. Yet these feelings are not our own and this section of the book helps you to address that. And, perhaps, to take time to reassess what your own thoughts and feelings are – without all of the external noise.

Clingy Babies

When your babies are 'clingy'
And whining is all they seem to do,
Would you try to think of it,
As them taking care of you?
Wait give me a minute,
Let me clarify what I mean.
We need to rest
To be our best
But that time of rest, seems wasteful
When the fridge is empty
And the sink is full
And other mums
Seem to do it all.

So baby boy
Or baby girl,
Attuned to a different way of life,
Can see our efforts and how we strive
And picks a time
An hour or two
Or maybe even a week
To slow us down

And cuddle with them
And give us time to breathe
Before
Once again
We're back up, doing it all
But they've given us time to rest with them
They saved us from a fall.
So 'clingy' babies are pretty awesome
The whining, not so much
But change the way you think about it
It's all done out of love.

Be Alive-Alive

In a world full of expectations
And stereotypes
The one thing I wish to leave behind,
Is a lesson I hold dear, from deep inside,
I wish to teach,
My girls
And the world,
Not to hide,
Who they truly are,
And not to lie
To themselves
Or others
Because they lack pride.
They must be alive
Alive-Alive
And their presence
Be it small
Or vast and wide
Has got to be full -
All encompassing
For them,
Inside
"Because it's not about the world

And what they think of you
Because it's not about the world
And what it thinks you should do"

It's about you

Your spirit
Alight with joy
Because
 You.

Because you
Are true
To you.

Not Unseen

Unshaven
Unshrunk
But not unseen.
The body of a goddess
The shape of a queen.

In all of the realness
I'm building my self esteem
And who would have thought
That a place like Instagram
With the beautiful, the artsy, the curated feeds,
Could work to create a new sense of self love
And belief.

I'm seven months postpartum,
The second time,
And I look five months pregnant
Every night.
Now I could show you my figure, wrapped in
clothes,
And I could twist this way and that, to find the
perfect pose,
But I'd much rather strip down,

And get real with myself,

And tell you, that for the sake of our (collective) mental health,

The bullshit about 'snap back' is a belief to be dropped,

It's rarely realistic and it needs to stop.

Our minds are overflowing with all of this chatter,

Other people's thought chip away at us

As they batter our brains

And shape our beliefs

So here's to reclaiming our minds

Here's to finally being free

Here's to wholeheartedly being ourselves

And not being unseen.

Labels

The labels.
 They don't define you.
They may,
For a fleeting moment,
Describe you.
But you are a human being;
Always growing,
Always changing
And
Always entitled
To change your mind,
To change your beliefs
To change your behavior.

For a while
You may decide
 That the way you were raised
 Is how you'd wish
 To raise your child,
 And then something happens,
Then there is a shift
And you decide
You wish

To do things a little different.
Very different.
That's okay.

You may decide
 That you will sleep train,
 Against all the well-meaning advice,
 Because being a gentle parent is ... taking its toll
on you.
That's okay.
You may,
After a few nights
Or even a few minutes,
Change your mind.
That's okay too.

You may wish
To live
 And / or
 Parent
 In a way that you have never ever seen before,
 In a way that feels just right to you.
That you can do.
That you should do!

Regardless

Of the sideways looks

That you're going to get,

 Because

Let's be honest

You are going to get looked at

Sideways,

Upwards

And down upon

By others who don't understand,

Who don't experience life the same way that you

do.

 We live in a judgmental world.

 But you're free to do what you want to do*

 And if what you're doing

 Is out of love

 And/ or

 For sanity's sake

 You're most likely doing the best thing for

yourself

 And your family too

 Even

 When it looks very different from what

'everyone' else is doing.

A Lot More Love

As the days slowly unfold before me I see my
girls rapidly grow and change. It's wild because
within the space of one day one or both of them
can become quite a different little lady.

As the days slowly unfolded before her, she
watched as her babies grew and changed. She
felt a sense of wildness. In the space of one day,
one or both of her babies could become quite
different little people.
She thought back to when it was only her eldest,
who was still just a little lamb chop. The days
were even slower then.
She paid attention to every little detail, noticed
every pitch change. She knew what to expect
when (according to the books, according to the
apps).

This time around, there were two. There was
real wildness. There was a lot more winging it
and divided attention.

Once upon a time she'd have felt bad, guilty even. When she mothered an only child she longed for a sibling for her baby to play with. Now she had one, and they loved it.

The guilt though, it lingered. It made her worry that her newest baby did not have her undivided attention, not like the first time she became a mother.

She spoke out into the open, "you bitch," she said, addressing guilt. "My attention may be divided, but my love is not. And as for my babies, well, they'll have their sibling's time and love to make up for it."

My Body

Under my clothes
The reality
Lies,
My body
Will never be the same.

And why should it,
For I will never be the same.
I was once a girl,
Carefree and careless,
Reckless!
I am now a mother,
Full of worries and hopes
But most of all,
Love.
My mother marks may or may not fade away,
But within each one,
Is written a story of expansion,
A story of growth,
The ultimate story of love.
Not for one second
 Do I wish it

That my body goes 'back' to being what it once
was.

No,
Not for a single moment!

My only hope
Is that I am
Always grateful
For the job well done by this body of mine,
That I remember to read these markings as a
story of love.
To remind myself that these marks have not
ruined me,
They have not tainted my body,
They've made me a mother and that is all.

My body will do what it wants moving
'forward'
And I will honour that.
I've never been too hung up on having the
perfect body
And to be honest,
I don't ever wish it on myself to be that way...
Because I already have the *perfect* body

- I've got a beating heart,
A fully functional brain
And lungs full of glorious air!

Oh, I guess that means your body is perfect too?!

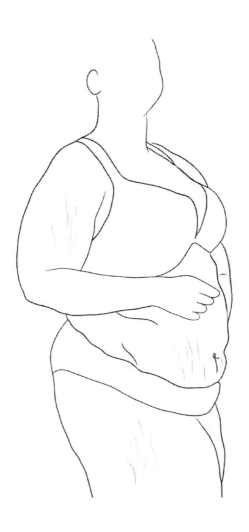

Unwell

When you're unwell
Just like that
All my worries disappear
And my attention sits with us
It sits with us right here
I can feel your presence next to me
Buzzing away
 Ever so gently
I can hear you breathing
 Deeply
Your skin,
It's hot to touch
Oh, my little love,
You need me

So I will cease to do all the things
The tidying,
 The cooking
And rushing
I will slow down,
 Help you get cool
And then nothing,
Nothing at all

But soothe you
And love you,
More than I have ever loved
You.

Soon you'll feel better my little babe,
And until then,
The rest of the world can wait.

Mantra

I've got my whole life to make up for this.

On Auto

And just for a moment,
I'd like for the noise to stop.
I'd like for the notifications to mute themselves
I'd like for the need to check my phone to cease.
I'd like to paint, or write, to bake, to create.

I'd like to take up space
Add something to this world
I'd like for my day to be just that,
My day
To make of it and to mould just the way *I* please.

I'd like to choose to do something that I really
want to do
I'd like, just for one day, one moment even, to be
free from the me I've been.

Gratitude

In *Gratitude* I examine those small moments of pure bliss. *Gratitude* is about every time you smiled at your child(ren) and watched them while they slept. *Gratitude* is every time your heart grew a little more.

I've placed these words part way through the book because we're on a journey. The layout of the book is intended to show that gratitude is something neither only at the beginning nor the end of motherhood; but rather is present throughout.

It's even present in the small moments that we so often overlook. So please, slow down – and take a look.

Co-Sleeping

I am in my happy place
Hopefully I'll be asleep soon
But while I'm awake
This moment I will take
To savour this perfection
That is you two.

My boobs feel empty
But that's okay
My girls and my bed are full.

One snores softly
Down by my feet
The other
Farts tunes into the sheets

And that is all it takes
For me to feel great
For me to feel
Grateful.

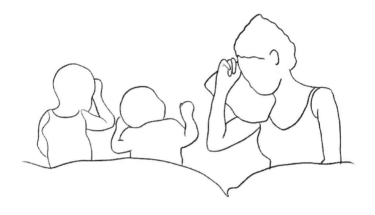

Someone Close By

The winters are no longer cold and dark. They're brightened with a warmth that only sticky little fingers and high-pitched squeals can bring. There's always someone close by to care for, to look at and laugh with; someone to wake you up at night - when it's silent. And the silence, when you choose to listen to it, brings a peace to fill your heart for a thousand days.

Jasmine and Ocean

Flow over everything

Like the waves of the ocean

Or the scent of the jasmine

Clothes in the Bath

And it was when she found herself sitting fully clothed in an empty bathtub with the shower curtain drawn, that she realised she'd lost something of herself. Hiding from children, really?

She knew that on so many levels this was normal. For nothing she ever did was new under the sun. But she wondered anyway, who else was out there hiding from their children like this? Who else would get caught because they were sniggering too loudly at the sheer confusion of their children looking for them in the unlikeliest of places?

"Look in Mr. Teddy's backpack."

'Really? Would I, could I really fit in Mr. Teddy's backpack?' She thought to herself as she let out a snort.

It's hilarious. The children are hilarious and she loved them with all of her soul. But those five unpeaceful minutes. Those five minutes in the bath, behind the shower curtain was necessary.

"There she is!"

The littlest squeals.

"Here I am!"

And she began it all again.

The First Breath

And it was in that moment that I could breathe
again
I'd been breathing this whole time,
Of course,
But it was strained
And bedraggled
And I hadn't noticed

But when I decided
That I didn't care anymore
That I'm going to relax
Into the moment
And into the unfolding of life
I sort of became
Me.

I became free
That's all I know
I actually breathed
And it felt so soothing
It felt real
I didn't have to think about it
I didn't have to think about

Anything
I just went with it
And it flowed

Like actually flowed
For real

I'd thought I'd experience flow before
But this
This was flow on another level
And it came, simply because I decided
…
To have it;
Really.

I am Mother

You came along
A tiny force to be reckoned with
And you changed me
You changed my name

Now
I am yours
I am

Mother

Me Time

I stay awake late
After I've put the girls to bed
Not long - sometimes an hour
Sometimes less
But I value that time
To focus on my goals
To focus on myself
To make reparations
And
For my mental health

Then,
Throughout the night
One will wake up
One will go down
And on and on
Until I'm worn down
And the morning light
Streams through the night
And the day
Another day
Has begun.

Alight

My soul is alight tonight
Watching you both sleep

I am the luckiest mother in the world
I tell myself,
Although it's been a tough week

I look at you from left to right
From right to left
And back

I gaze for a moment at your tiny curls
And then, your chubby cheeks
Your lips are squished against the bed
And your fingers curl and twitch
You noisily but softly breathe
And
 I find myself at peace

There's nothing more
That matters now
Than this moment
We have here

You're snug and warm
You're safe and sound
You're sleeping side by side

And my mother heart
 It fills with love,
My heart is full of pride.

Goodnight my girls
I love you both
I pray your dreams are bliss
I cannot wait until the morning, now
To wake you with a kiss.

Cuddles

Reminiscing

She cried a little during their cuddle. She cried because that was the only way she could get a cuddle anymore. When her baby girl had fallen asleep. She'd bend over her, cooing, as she watched her sleep. She'd scoop her up off of the sofa, pull her daughter's limp arms around her neck and walk her to the bedroom. She'd linger a little too long, deciding if it had been long enough. It was never long enough. So she stood and cuddled her more. She let the tears fall silently down her face thinking of all the days she had wished away. Nostalgic for the hot and sticky summers when she begged her toddler to stop climbing on her. She'd smile at the memories. She'd snigger, because now - now, it was the other way around. "Leave me, Mummy, I'm busy!" she'd been told, all too often.

'She's growing up way too quickly and it hurts my heart a little bit,' she'd often think. And, no word of a lie, her heart always came inches away from breaking. 'It hurts because she's not going to be this little forever,' she'd continue conversing with herself. 'But, you've got to stop looking back, stop the pain.' That's what her therapist had told her, 'You stop looking back if it makes you feel this way. You've got a whole beautiful, dream of a future to look forward to.'

She put her baby down in bed, sat beside her and took out her journal and pen.

Resolving

I'll gaze at her,
My little muse,
I'll cradle her while she sleeps,
And even when it hurts my back,
I'll be grateful for a squeeze.

I'll wipe away her tears
When she cries,
Listen to the way she breathes,
I'll relish the twinkle in her eye
When she comes home
Back to me.

I'll dance with her every morning
 To her nonsensical but magical songs.
I'll teach her to be an amazing human,
Big sister, and friend,
And I'll leave the washing and the laundry
When she asks me to be a zombie - again

Dear Postpartum Body

You are so beautiful
And I am absolutely mesmerised
By you.
How you've changed,
The stories you tell,
You have grown
Not one, but two
Little human beings
And I am so proud of you

And I continue to rely on you,
We all do,
To sustain life,
To do what you do,
To regenerate your cells
And to keep us all well
To adapt and protect
To forgive and accept
The pressure I put you through

'They' may not think you're perfect now
But I do
You're beautiful
And I love you.

Children

Seeing you together

Four hands

Twenty little fingers

Grasping on to each other

Evokes a smile deep down in my heart

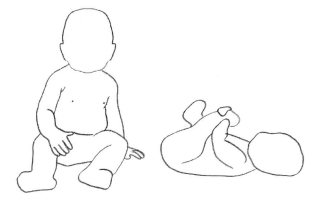

Solidarity

Thus far all the words and emotions have been mine.

Solidarity though represents the same truths but from the perspectives of others.

At the end of this collection you'll find some blank pages where you can write your own feelings.

Thinking and writing is an amazing way to come to terms with the emotions represented in *Fluctuation* and the advice offered in *Perspectives*. It also immortalises the joy we draw from moments of *Gratitude*.

My Equal

You are my equal

A little sequel

But with a story

Of your very own.

And so

No matter your feelings,

Your choices,

Your age

I'll love and respect you

I'll create a space

For your feelings

And

For your voice

And I'll always strive to teach you joy

Gratitude

Love

And peace.

Welcome,

My littlest love,

Welcome to the world.

- inspired by Mimi Ikonn

Actual Love

She may never have understood what love meant. Not if it wasn't for her baby.

She'd resolved that not having an option to run, when she felt she needed to run had taught her how to become a new woman. It defined, for her, what it meant to be a mum. Unconditional, sacrificial love. She grew so strong in those moments of struggle. So strong! She grew even more deeply rooted in a love she never knew she was capable of possessing.

She found patience in the impatience; solutions in the conundrums of life; and she finally found love. Actual love. Love. Love for another person, Love. It was mind blowing because she had never been able to find any for herself. This love though, it was something seriously special. It must have been made of the same stuff as magic.

She knew that this was her forever and so, more than ever, she was determined to make forever magical, for him.

- inspired by Carrie-Anne

rror

It was those who were closest
That made comment after comment
About what they didn't like
About what they'd do differently
About how they wish they could change things.
About how they wished that could change me.

It was awful
Having all of my fear
Appear
Before me.
They were supposed to be
My loved ones
My family.
But
I wasn't enough.
I was too much.
It was confirmed.

And now,
This unbelievable fear
Of being weighed,
Measured,

Edited and adapted

Was something I had to strip away,

From me

For my baby

Because now my insecurities would play out

Through me

Upon my baby.

And, as if looking in a mirror

I'd create a beautiful, terrified little person.

-     inspired by Becky Robinson

Always Enough

Sometimes I feel frustrated
Motherhood seems all consuming
Sometimes I feel like I've got this
Sometimes it's so confusing

Sometimes I feel like I'm the only one
Losing against the tantrums
Sometimes I feel like I'm already done
And chaos is a personal anthem

Sometimes I look at others
Their motherhood looks immaculate
Sometimes I look at my family
And have to remind myself to value it

Sometimes exhaustion takes over and I can
barely even function
And I get really close to believing that I've
already begun to malfunction

Sometimes I feel touched out
Sometimes I feel so smothered
Sometimes I take a break

And technology helps me to mother

Sometimes I wish my old life back
As I second guess my ability
And wonder if I am cut out for this job
Because it's so hard mentally and physically

But always you look at me and love me,
Always.
Every day the same.
You look at me with eyes of love
And peel away the shame
You look at me and smile with love
And in those moments, I know,
I am enough - always enough
The way *you* love, it shows.

- inspired by Maria Betsworth

Role Model Mother

Look at me,
Baby,
Look at me and see
That the whole wide world
Is within our reach

And this moment right here
As we look out at sea
Is here so you know
That it's within your reach,
It's within your power
To live, to be free

Look at me,
Baby,
Look and believe,
I'm living truth, proof
That dreams
Don't only unfold during our sleep

And this moment right here
As we soar through the sky
Is truly magical

Do you know why?
This is the place
Where you learn your worth
Is defined by you
And your connection to the earth

Look at me,
Baby,
Look at what we've achieved,
We've taken the world by the hand
And danced among trees

And this moment right here
As I watch you drift off to sleep
Is here so I know
I'm doing the right thing

-       inspired by Sunshine Abou Bakar

Her Heart

Their world was full
Of affirmations
Symbols
Carnations
About who they were,
About who they might become,
About their power.
Thus,
They had already won.

And although they were only young,
They were already crowned
Kings and queens
In her heart.

The world had nothing,
Nothing on her heart.

- inspired by Africa Daley-Clarke

NO ONE
BELONGS
HERE MORE
THAN YOU!

Affirmations

I'm art
I'm sexy
I've birthed three children
I breastfeed

The dark
It gets me
But I'm no longer afraid
So I'm free

I'll start
Accepting
I'm worthy
Of the best things

I'll laugh
Daily
Mind, body and soul
Healthy

I'll love
All of me
I'll trust myself
My integrity

I've experienced
Many things
But motherhood is the most
Transforming

- inspired by Lillian Jamfar

Mother of the Modern Day

She rose up,
Like a phoenix
Out of the ashes
Of the ages
Past

She shook the boundaries
And kicked them down
And as they crashed into the ground
She raised her voice
Above the noise

To remain quiet now,
She had no choice
Because she was
And
She was a mother
To a little black girl
Who would look around
And see
That the world was not for her

And possibly
Shaking in fear,
Retreat right there
Never to be heard of,
Her story never shared,
As patriarchy
And white supremacy
Would lead the way
For evermore

No!
That was not okay,
She was not a mother
Of the modern day
To leave things as they were
To discourage change

She would fight
To see the light of day,
The break of dawn,
Another way,
She would fight,
She would fight away

She was her Why.

Her baby girl
Deserved the world
And it would be hers
One day
Her story would be shared
She'd never live in fear
And in every win that she would have
An echo we will hear
An echo of her empowered voice
Would be heard,
Saying,
Now I have a choice
And that's because
You've paved the way
And changed the days
For me.

Thank You, Mum

-    inspired by Candice Brathwaite

For your musings

Printed in Great Britain
by Amazon

38502477R00061